WHY DOES IRON TASTE FUNNY?

Chemistry Book for Kids 6th Grade
Children's Chemistry Books

In this book, we're going to talk about the uses and importance of the element of iron. So, let's get right to it!

26
55.845
Fe
[Ar]3d⁶4s²
Iron

THE FACTS ABOUT IRON

Iron is a metal that is hard, yet brittle. The abbreviation for iron in the periodic table is Fe, which comes from the word for iron in Latin—"ferrum." Its atomic number is 26 and therefore it has 26 protons or positive charges.

At room temperature it's a solid and is a grayish metal that is somewhat soft. Its density is about 7.9 grams per cubic centimeter, which is much less dense than gold. It melts at 2,800 degrees Fahrenheit and it boils at 5,181.8 degrees Fahrenheit.

iron ore

In a list of elements that are most abundant throughout the universe, it would be the second most abundant metal, after

aluminum, and the sixth most abundant element overall.

Iron has 33 different isotopes. Isotopes are atoms of the same element that have the same number of electrons and protons, but a different number of neutrons. Four of those are stable isotopes that occur naturally. They include 54Fe, 56Fe, 57Fe, and 58Fe with 56Fe being the most abundant.

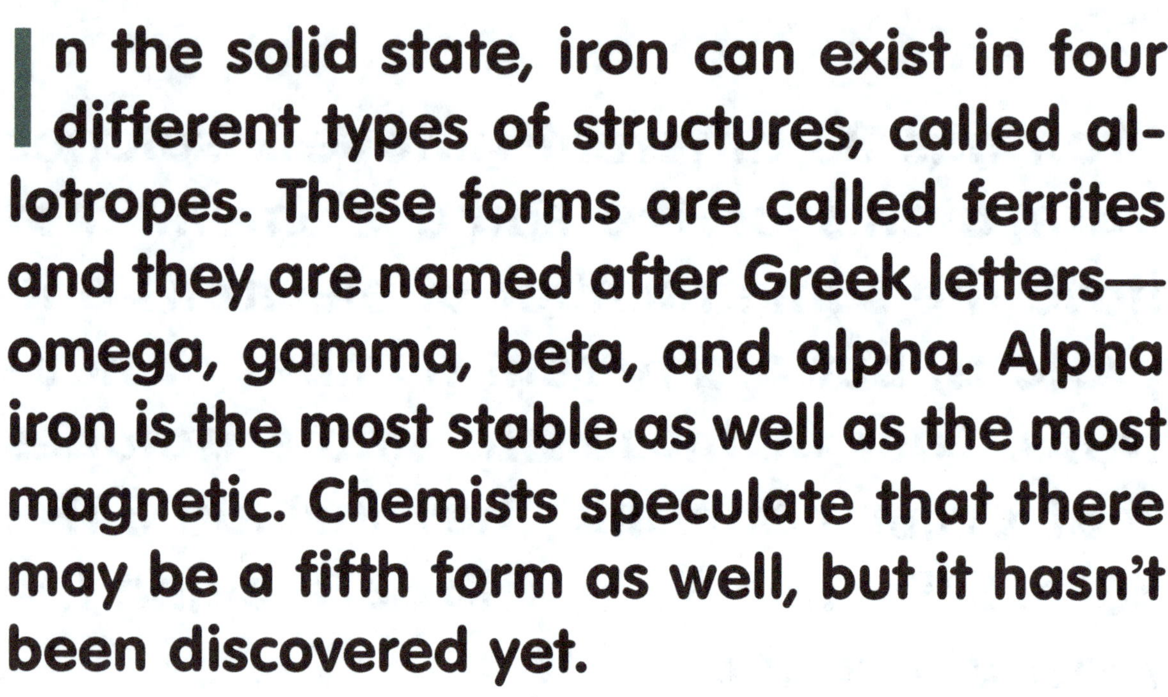

In the solid state, iron can exist in four different types of structures, called allotropes. These forms are called ferrites and they are named after Greek letters—omega, gamma, beta, and alpha. Alpha iron is the most stable as well as the most magnetic. Chemists speculate that there may be a fifth form as well, but it hasn't been discovered yet.

iron sand

magnet with iron powder

CHARACTERISTICS OF IRON

Like gold, it's also a transition metal, but unlike gold, it's not very dense and it's very reactive. It easily corrodes and rusts when exposed to oxygen. Because it's malleable, it can conduct both heat as well as electricity fairly well. Of all the elements, iron has the most natural magnetism and iron filings are sometimes used in magnetic games.

HOW IS IRON USED?

Iron is relatively soft by itself, but when carbon is added to it, steel is the result. Steel is used to make everything from paperclips to skyscrapers. Steel is an alloy made up of iron with about 1% carbon. Sometimes steel includes other elements as well, such as manganese, but it's primarily made of iron.

steel sheets

iron ore mining

After aluminum, iron is the most abundant metal in the Earth's crust. In a list of the most abundant elements in Earth's crust, it's ranked 4th and makes up about 5% of the crust.

Scientists believe that much of the inner core of the Earth is made of iron. Iron is highly reactive and oxidizes when it's exposed to the air. For this reason, most of the iron that is found on Earth's surface is in hematite and magnetite, which are iron oxide minerals. It can also be extracted from limonite as well as taconite and siderite.

Iron is also found in abundance in the Sun and other stars.

hematite

iron meteorite

HOW LONG HAVE PEOPLE BEEN USING IRON?

Archaeological evidence proves that people were using iron as early as 4000 BC. They used it to make tools, various types of weapons, and other objects. At the beginning, they got this iron from meteorites.

The word "iron" comes from an ancient Anglo-Saxon word that means "metal from the sky." When the explorer Admiral Robert Peary went to Greenland during the late 1800s, the native people there, called the Inuit, had been making tools from iron they extracted from a meteorite that had fallen there 300 years before.

Robert Peary

hoba iron meteorite

Archaeologists have also found iron beads made by the ancient Egyptians that carbon date to around 3200 BC. The iron for these beads was also extracted from meteorites. Passages in the Old Testament of the Bible mention men who work with iron.

It's not known when people learned how to extract iron from ore. By 1200 BC, iron ore was mixed with charcoal, a form of carbon, and turned into masses of hot material.

Iron metal was then forged from this material by hammering. The more it was put into the fire with the burning charcoal, the harder the material became. This was

the beginning of the manufacture of steel. The time period of history between 1200 BC to 500 BC is called the Iron Age.

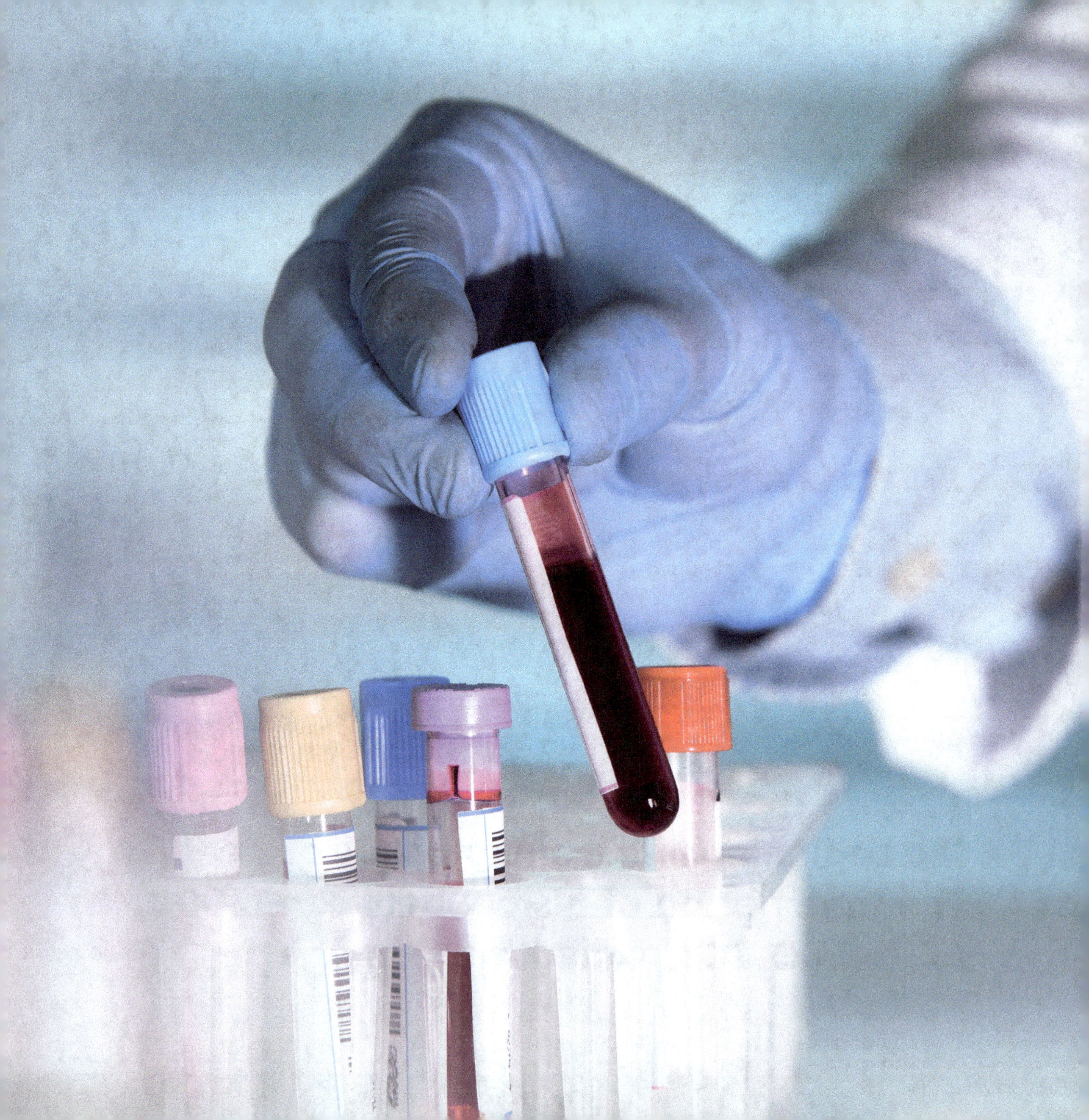

WHY DOES IRON TASTE FUNNY?

Have you ever tasted iron? You might not think you have, but if you've ever tasted your own blood after you've cut yourself, then you've tasted iron. The taste has been described as bitter, coppery, metallic, rusty, and salty. Just like everyone's sweat is different, everyone's blood is different too.

WHY IS IRON IMPORTANT TO LIVING CREATURES?

Iron is critical to the well being of tiny underwater bacteria that use CO2 for the process of photosynthesis. These bacteria are called phytoplankton.

phytoplankton

algae

Some scientists believe that pumping extra iron into ocean water could help curtail excess carbon dioxide. But, others have argued that by doing this we would begin the growth of algae that produce toxins and thereby contaminate marine life.

Iron is also a critical nutrient for animals and human beings. If you have a deficiency of iron, you can get very tired because it causes anemia. Having anemia means you're not as strong when performing physical tasks.

Fe

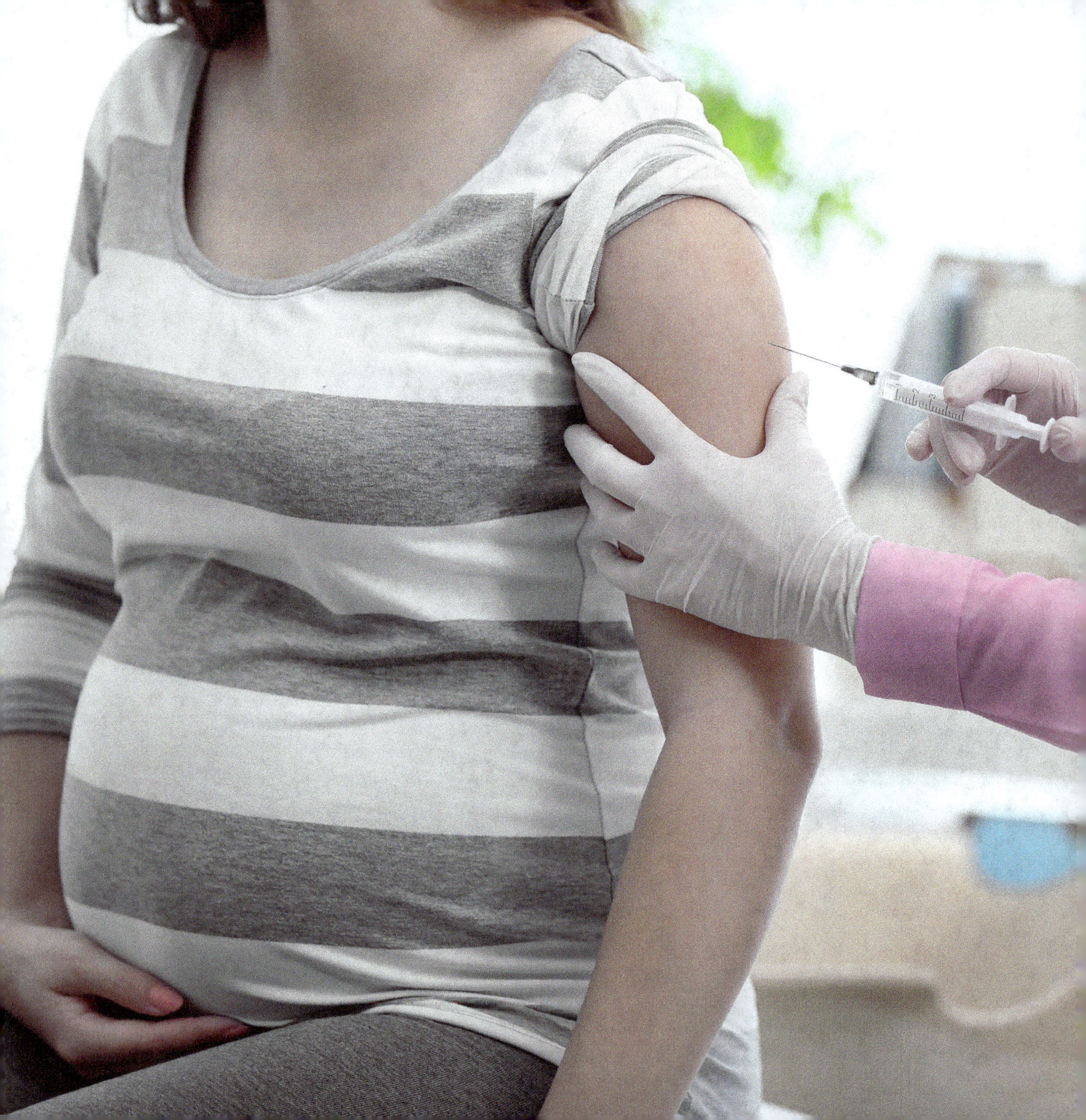

Iron deficiency can also cause weakened memory capacity as well as weakened mental function, especially for teenagers. Women who are anemic while pregnant are at risk for giving birth to premature, underweight babies.

There are two types of iron that are important to get in your diet. Heme iron is the easiest for the body to absorb. It's found in red meat, poultry, and seafood. Non-heme iron, which is also absorbed by the body, just not as readily, can be found in dark green vegetables, such as spinach, broccoli, and kale as well as meats.

If you consume something that contains vitamin C like citrus fruits or tomato juice while you're eating foods with non-heme iron, it will increase the absorption of the iron.

As with all types of nutrients, the proper balance of iron in the body is very important. Too little iron is a problem, but so is too much iron. Iron can be toxic to the body in large doses. There's medical evidence that people who have too much heme-iron in their blood can be more susceptible to heart disease. Also, too much iron has also been linked to Alzheimer's disease.

old man with alzheimer's disease

S275
stainless steel

HOW IS IRON USED TODAY?

Today, most iron is used to make steel, which is an alloy of iron mixed with carbon. The stainless steel that is used for appliances, cookware, and "silverware" is about 10% chromium, which helps it to be resistant to rust, the major problem with iron in its pure state. Sometimes other elements are added to iron to give it additional characteristics.

Adding nickel makes the resulting steel more durable as well as resistant to acids and prolonged heat. The addition of manganese to steel also adds durability and tungsten as an additive helps steel retain its strength and hardness even at very high temperatures. You can't go anywhere without being surrounded by steel in buildings, cars, ships, and planes.

nickel mineral

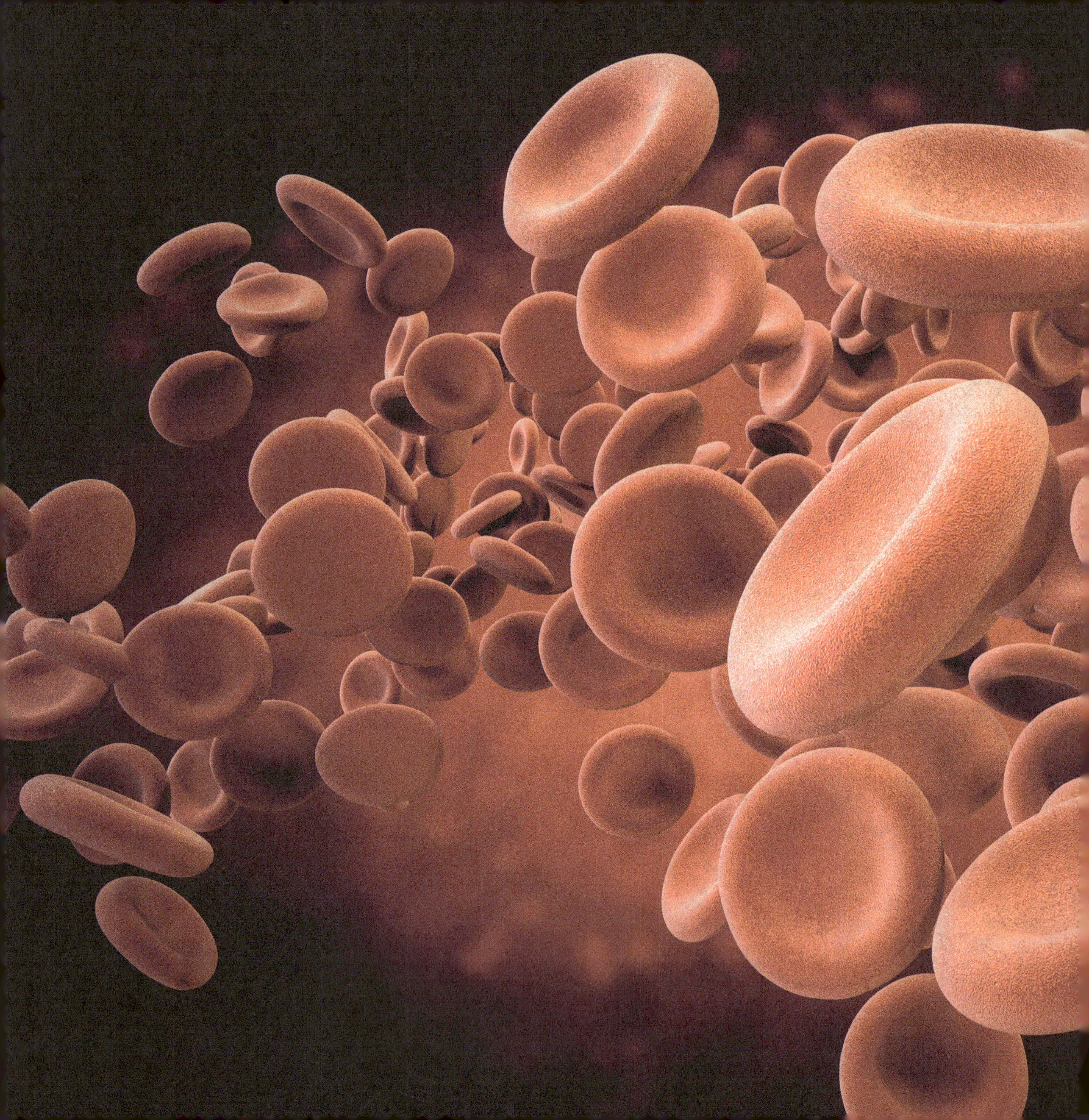

FASCINATING FACTS ABOUT IRON

There's an iron pillar still standing in India that dates back to 400 AD. Despite the fact that iron corrodes quickly, this pillar has survived probably due to the other metals mixed with the iron.

Our blood is a red color due to the way iron mixes with oxygen. The chemical bonds between the two elements reflect light.

We think of iron as something strong and unbreakable but pure iron is soft and somewhat malleable. However, when iron is mixed with carbon and other elements it becomes steel, which is very strong.

About 90% of the metal on Earth that is being extracted and refined today is iron.

steel tubes

cast iron skillet

The meteorites called siderites are largely composed of iron.

Cast iron was invented in China around the 5th century BC. Iron is heated to a liquid form and carbon is added to it. It is poured into a mold and when it cools it is a cast-iron object. Many people still use cast-iron skillets in their kitchens.

teel is sometimes so hard that it is one thousand times as hard as pure iron.

Iron is found in abundance on other rocky planets and celestial bodies besides Earth.

At any given time, an average man's body contains about 3.8 grams of iron and the average woman has about 2.3 grams.

steel mill

Mars

The red color of the planet Mars is due to iron oxidizing and forming rust. In Ancient times, objects made with iron were used for ceremonial purposes. It was too expensive to use for everyday life. It replaced bronze and was used more commonly during the Iron Age.

Awesome! Now you know more about the uses of iron and how important iron is to our bodies. You can find more Chemistry books from Baby Professor by searching the website of your favorite book retailer.

Visit
BABY PROFESSOR
EDUCATION KIDS
www.BabyProfessorBooks.com
to download Free Baby Professor eBooks and view
our catalog of new and exciting Children's Books